GALLOWGLASS

GALLOWGLASS

SUSAN TICHY

BOISE STATE UNIVERSITY • BOISE • IDAHO • 2010

Ahsahta Press, Boise State University
Boise, Idaho 83725-1525
http://ahsahtapress.boisestate.edu
http://ahsahtapress.boisestate.edu/books/tichy2/tichy2.htm

Library of Congress Cataloging-in-Publication Data
Tichy, Susan, 1952-
 Gallowglass / Susan Tichy.
     p. cm. -- (The new series ; no. 34)
 Poems.
 ISBN-13: 978-1-934103-13-5 (pbk. : alk. paper)
 ISBN-10: 1-934103-13-6 (pbk.)
 I. Title.
 PS3570.I26G36 2010
 811'.54--DC22

                              2009042544

ACKNOWLEDGMENTS

Grateful acknowledgment is offered to the editors & staff of journals who first published some of these poems: *42opus* for "A Visit to the Underworld Can Permanently Alter Your Perspective on 'Restless Existence'"; *Agni* for "Predator" & "American Ghazals"; *Beloit Poetry Journal,* for "'The Reflection of Black Is Never Black, But Pure Dark Green'" (there titled "Implicature"), "One, Two," "Book Land Night," & "Stork"; *Denver Quarterly* for "Lead Belly" & "Trebuchet"; *Free Verse* for "'My Brother's Name Is Babylon'" & "No Copied Species Are Fooled"; *Indiana Review* for "Gallowglass"; *Luna* for "Song Found Among Words" & "Dissertations Have Been Ruined by the Mockingbird"; *Practice: New Writing +Art* for "Summer Is Brief" & "Readable Means"; *Runes* for "Ice or Salt".

For tea, conversation, and editorial pencils, warm thanks to Lesley Smith, Margaret Yocom, Adrian Lurssen, Alec Finlay, Joan Wilcox, Mel Nichols, Jennifer Atkinson, Zofia Burr, Allison Cobb, Jennifer Coleman, Peter Streckfus, and Caroline Walker. Special thanks to Danika Myers, for putting the horse back in front of the cart; and to Tuyet-Hoa Hoang, who prescribed the dictionary as a palliative for grief.

To my trail companions: I wish you good feet.

FOR MICHAEL, ONE MORE

. . . but everything personal soon rots; it must be packed in ice or salt.

W. B. Yeats

CONTENTS

GALLOWGLASS

1.

Three men who look like Bedouin, but are not, pause with their camels in the snow—
Photo shot through a bus window, twenty-nine years ago on the Khyber Pass.

On the radio I thought they said, 'The way the war is disinfected,'
So I turned the page over and found it blank.

Was. Was. Was. Was, the mad poet said. But the president says no,
That poet wasn't mad. That poet understood the rent collector.

Rats run closely along a wall, the wall and body always touching.
If you tear the wall down, rats run closely along the wall's memory.

Flight here uneventful, homicide movie in the main cabin.
A soldier is writing a story about a soldier writing a story.

Who is afraid? An axe cuts branches, can't cut leaves.
Wild strawberry not yet bloomed, wild geranium tangled in the monkshood.

In all the photographs, something particular lies in the lower foreground:
A bare foot or a water jug, a soldier's pocket, a cell phone, a gun.

Something is red on the floor, I can't see what. A bit of sunlight crosses a prisoner's arm.
'The other truth has disappeared, as if it didn't exist.'

Strange headlights in the driveway, and the father of the first dead soldier says,
'Dog barking three a.m.: there they are.'

2.

The guards wear helmets with plastic shields drawn down over their faces.
The prisoners wear white hoods with black circles drawn to replace their faces.

On the cover of a glossy book, a soldier from my home town uses his rifle to push a crowd
Farther away from the camera. Street noise used as a painter uses paint.

My ancestors were prisoners of war, transported to a colony where half died in the first year.
Their children bought black slaves and became white.

In the foreground, bodies half wrapped in cloth, in shadow. And farther back,
Behind the black figure of the grieving woman, a pile of white bundles in the sun.

In a sandy ditch, army scouts found the body of a Sioux woman. Shot in the throat,
She had bled so much her foot looked to them like the foot of a white man.

Oil is black. Salt is white. Unless we unwrap the bodies it doesn't matter.
Once we unwrap the bodies it doesn't matter.

He identified the dead because he had to, then he zipped them back into their bags.
For thirty years that zip so loud he couldn't piss in a public place.

Between the words *man held captive* and the words *stands bound*
Are twelve words of army-speak and a lot of white paint worn off the wall.

When refugees ask directions, say yes. Clean salt from shoes. White paint
Over red paint. Conventional forms of lions and the bridge burns all night.

3.

Because I was trying to eat less, I woke up hungry in the middle of the night.
Distant, bloody, tedious, my radio said, and in that order.

Exhibit of work by photographers killed in the war. It is black and white, Hanoi is rainy,
Our plane is leaving, and one of the dead has a daughter here wiping her eyes.

When they interviewed a soldier, he said, 'I didn't think anything.'
A rocket slammed into the sixth floor, out of a helicopter or out of a donkey cart.

Simple black shape of a woman stands posed between a camera and a tank,
Well-dressed children artfully framed by a soldier's elbow and his gun.

Some of the dead were mercenaries. Helmeted soldiers cry in the street.
Mad poet stamps and whirls, says every death is one, one, one, one, one.

Open a book. Watch *harbor* turn to *harry, army, barrow, borough,*
A fortified town, a room with a closed door.

I am buying bread when the war begins. The baker, who has never talked to me before,
Teaches me the word for *oppose*. He says, 'Is this how you feel?'

The girders are green, the sky is clear, the burned bodies hang from orange cords.
In barracks, soldiers play video games and bang their fists on the air conditioners.

Sleep is a cure for wakefulness, I'm told. My first night home I don't go in.
I lie down between the cactus and the pines.

4.

Beaver-cut trees in an aspen grove. Cutthroat trout in pond shadow.
Listening to lies on the radio all morning.

There's a grammar for those who are in the room, and a grammar for those who aren't.
When a tank shoots through a brick wall, a little piano riff in a minor key.

On a shelf above the television, one toy cyclo cut from a beer can, red and white *33*.
Training jets in pairs buzz low, stampede horses through the barbed-wire fences.

In Hanoi I bought no souvenirs. In Saigon I bought a white stone dragon
Packed in a box with a pool of red ink.

Five cans of gasoline, two small boys, riding together in a blue cart.
If you fire shots into the air the boy in the green shirt winces.

In a notebook, my list of belongings: I wanted to leave each thing to its rightful heir.
When you walk against wind in a sandstorm, shield your eyes and cover your teeth.

The man with the gun is standing up. The man without a gun is lying down.
The car is red and white, the sky is blue, the building brown.

I asked what the woman in black was searching for. She said
For scissors, with which to cut one lock of his precious hair.

When the tree fell, we were lying asleep in grass near the beaver ponds.
This is why I can say that we were spared.

1.

Today another helicopter crashed. Today another tank drove over a cut-bank unto death.
'Likes to meet with potentates,' said John Dean on the radio. 'Doesn't like to kiss babies.'

I imagine a lover's arm lying between my breasts. All right so far,
But how would I advertise it?

Voice says, 'Mural on the water tower,' or 'Wilde gees hihe in the ayer vp fleen,'
While two men sit on a park bench, watch sparrows pick dead bugs from the grilles of cars.

Here is the photograph: my husband and a tour guide in front of the victory mural, Revolutionary
Museum, Saigon. He has bowed his head, as if he were reading a caption down by his knees.

Impetuous. Firebrand. Persistent. Surprise. In several towns claimed as their own.
Or so it says here. Says here, that Revolution City is a slum.

I went in to buy a nifty pen and came out with 47 dollars & 62 cents worth
Of something that weighed about 15 pounds.

Small copperhead coiled and sleepy, strikes at me with a pink tongue.
Bullet at twice the speed of sound can shatter an organ it does not touch.

Her eyes are down but her chin is high, as if she were carrying water on top of her head.
She walks away at an angle, and her shiny blue *ai dao* turns back my flash.

Fox lying dead on pavement—the only thing I remember in an eight-hour drive.
Walk to buy milk in a driving rain because—. I couldn't finish the sentence.

In fact, when I really look at this, he's headless, bent down so far between her back
And the mural's nearest point, its most detailed figures, that he simply disappears.

2.

In Viggo Mortensen's dead chant of Jonathan Swift's 'Holyhead,' guitar strings lull a sea
That can't be crossed. Glue what you're reading into this book so you can't disown it.

It's a poor-will calling in the scrub pine, a *ha'nt in the talk,* or a fury stuck on replay.
Kids in the street throw sheet glass. Spin. Strident. Larger Spin. Upstart or upwrath.

I went in to buy a nifty pen and came out with 38 dollars and 91 cents worth
Of something that weighed about 15 pounds and wasn't edible.

The sea is crossed by *wild geese,* not desire: ship with a belly full of exiles, puking their guts out
And hugging their hired guns. So what did he say to her? Nothing, except 'I was here before '75.'

Now Billy Bragg's uncooked guitar in a room with bad acoustics.
Betweenbetweenbetweenbetweenbetween if we aren't in one.

I imagine a lover's arm lying between, but it's no longer part of his body.
The dead are fair game while they lie in the street, though you can't photograph their coffins.

Next story: transmission of wealth and transmission of poverty both on the upswing.
Shined his gold teeth and his gold belt buckle. Name in block letters above the fold.

Shot in the ass, so his underwear shows its brand name all over the nightly news.
Killed a year after enlistment. No, it was less.

It was two o'clock on the twenty-fifth when I snapped this picture, in a French Colonial mansion,
With real chandeliers and floor wax and real tanks outside in the roses.

Tank coming in through the gate with its hatches down—that famous photo, that famous fake—
Hangs in the middle of the mural in a cheap black frame. Child's cry mistaken for a gull.

3.

Buck hits the glass with his velvet antlers, backflips over the hood, and survives the fall.
Street noise glued down to a plastic map and a stack of cinder blocks to hold up the gun.

Look up *mural* in the dictionary, and you wind up at *immure*.
Malaria drug caused panic attacks, but only after exposure to a dead Iraqi soldier.

His father was the only one in the family who died of wounds. 4-F, half blind, he insulated bombers.
Asbestos killed him twenty-three years after the war ended.

Newspapers stacked for wrapping fish. Boy with a sack of cans and a bloody lip.
Correction: exposure to a teenager machine-gunned in two.

I went in to buy a nifty pen and came out with one hundred twenty-two bucks worth
Of debt, a three-hole punch and some ersatz Snickers bars.

It's a simple truth: a helicopter choked by sand is not a combat casualty.
On the grand staircase, a wedding party posed for enough photographs to start a museum.

Voice on the radio says, 'Look at this.' Piano at one end of the stage, a red guitar at the other.
It's a beautiful photograph, he said, because all the people in it are alive.

Striations follow. One stratum of music is efficacy, one efficacy is granite beneath, against.
Then why doesn't he run, damnit? Why the hell doesn't he run?

Perfect. Lost. Unobtainable. A single tea tree called *Big Red Robe*.
And the plume of dust was beautiful, if you didn't think too hard about what it was.

Angry hummingbird hammers a scrub jay back and forth through brush for half an hour:
The luxury of choosing between predator and prey.

4.

So who was fighting and shedding the blood and who was just fucking around? I shackle:
Breaker One-Niner, helluva block One-Niner, Blue Swords and Resolved to Win. Unshackle.

Chewing gum. A flashlight. A partnership to remove trash.
But first a wild goose in an armored car passes from this bleakly shore.

So figure it out: *lying* versus *how the road lies*, and we don't know which is satire,
An actor selling stocks and bonds or the woman with an X of bloody bandage on her face.

The way I pictured it, a pastel street-scene of cheering women is angled out by the army-green
And red of the victory stuff, the tour guide in her blue dress bright and near.

O my husband, you silly goose. Eye of the cannon trained on the chandelier. I think that guitarist
Was Buckethead, with the sound of desire plugged in but the volume down.

I went in to buy a nifty pen and signed a check for 126 thousand 238 dollars & 19 cents
To pay some poor slob to drive a truck for a year in a desert country.

His black hand in a white hand, and it's either a lover's arm or a pressure bandage,
His cell phone tied to his chest with a green cord.

An angry man speaks English but they translate anyway.
Scarlet tanager bathing itself in a fast-running water.

Put a songbird nest in the mouth of a cannon. Tune the guitar like a bagpipe.
Ochre-colored Abrams tanks already lie dead in the gone-to.

His parents' house is surrounded now by satellite trucks and cameras.
Sound of a key as it opens the wrong lock.

LEAD BELLY

1.

Tail of a fish fans slowly, catches my eye, the rest of its body locked in the jaws
Of a copperhead, coiled back in rocks at the edge of a shallow lake.

Hot gun and a round cooked off through hip and thigh and bulkhead.
Valiant and hardy, burly of body, well-timbred all agreed.

The word *acrobats* on a playground, the word *door* on a fence. Across the border
Sunset dissects the hills with golden light.

'In rehab you become a piece of paper. The doctors write on it. That's what you are.'
Raise pitch, breathe, don't laugh.

Spanish guitar on electric guitar. On a white sheet a dark hand,
Its three fingers smooth and healed as glass.

Footsteps padding down the hall at night. Some beautiful brass some gray paint,
Gray plate to shield the gunner, with his trigger finger stomach heart.

Forty degrees below on the Khyber Pass,
Forty degrees below on the bare ridge where his ashes lie.

Children's bodies unclaimed in a morgue. Ankle rebuilt from part of his arm
So he walked on a foot and a half for thirty years.

Twenty-one soldiers killed themselves, but it took them a year and a half.
In a year and a half I could feel enough to feel bad.

'Checkpoint for the interim government.' 'Has withdrawn much of the statements it made.'
Fox sits still in the middle of the path for a moment before it runs.

2.

An old woman said to me, 'Hurt things come here,' and she didn't mean the bad art
Waiting in waiting rooms, paintings in which wild animals are a little too detailed and a lot too large.

Nostalgic flock of B-52s. A leg rebuilt from cadaver bone and metal.
'And our helicopter was dodging birds all the way to Baghdad.'

Some things you know immediately: 'twenty minutes until shock kills him,'
'Gray matter spilling out of his head,' and a pair of strange men at the widow's door.

We crossed that river on a beaver dam: his whole foot, his crippled foot, his grin,
While the only guy with two good hands takes step-by-step instructions on how to save a man's life.

Battalion moved five hundred yards in a day,
So write down a word and we'll call it *the point of attack.*

Camera a little too close to a cheekbone, face hidden by a microphone.
Graffiti here says *Rich Stench.* The singer rubs her thighs and can't sit still.

There's a kind of stunned afterglow, for minutes and then for years.
'Be taught by walking' was the best advice, but my one muddy boot left tracks across the carpet.

In his brain a piece of shrapnel the size of a quarter. In his house at the top of a steep path:
Rice, wild plants, and meat of a water buffalo killed by cold.

Soft parts triangulated, and a slur that makes him sound drunk.
He asked me to build a temple out of what I loved.

So which is it now, compadre? Sad and lonely, or sad and blue?
Eyes filled with dirt, and a salty smell he thought was the river was blood.

3.

Woody said, 'Leadbelly is a hard name,' and I've heard him sing a song about what happened.
Engineers blew a hole in the railroad berm, then the convoy *parked up* in a cemetery till dawn.

Dragon-eyed, pilotless airplanes. Disposable diapers on desert trails near the border,
And the baby was born on his bed though it wasn't his child.

In cross-section of a tree-trunk, a sapling the size of your finger is still the core.
Shell-casings fall in a readable pattern, but in no cross-section of a body can you find a child.

My mother's last words were *Never mind*, but I wrote them down anyway.
My feet are cold the pen is noisy, someone is banging metal at the house next door.

It's a state-of-the-art hospital, rocketed on the day it opened, or else a hopeless case of rock-n-roll.
Sunlight falls across my book, and some of the bodies were eaten by cats and dogs.

Mad poet says this is easy. Don't wear a stethoscope during an air raid.
Pause to admire the web design skills of whoever wrapped this text around an ad for a plasma t.v.

Hand hand, foot foot. Pen and paper wrapped in plastic, so no blood on them
That day they stoned him, rocked the van, broke windshield wipers off in their bare hands.

Girl with an umbrella running away. Boy without a mean bone in his body.
Graffiti in red says *people starve* and I photographed it through a chain link fence.

Women with heads covered, then blown off. Man with an artificial leg.
He's dead, so the doctors kept it, washed it in dish soap, used it again.

Laughing at inappropriate moments, burning his hand on the stove.
Scars on the back of his head the approximate rake of a lion's claws.

4.

The bass player said, 'You make a record from the bottom up.'
Pulling a legless man out of a truck and the ink still wet on his contract.

If part of your palm is burned away have you outlived fate?
It's not a truck, it's a tank, held upright by the bent prick of its own hot cannon.

I say *alexia*: word blindness. I say bottle of cooking oil with a dragon on it.
When he limped to the top of a mountain what did he see?

The javelina who gored my dog. Tattoo artist or a juggling act. A poem sandblasted on glass.
You can download any kind of violence you like.

We were hamming it up in the courtyard, posing for too many photographs
With a gun his boats could carry though they didn't carry this one.

Now it's one in the chest, two in the kidneys, laptop open on the baby grand
And reporters go in and out with the caravans.

I think what she sang was 'God Almighty's bread and cheese,'
Though it might have been *appease*.

Man wearing a baseball cap that reads *Big Sister*.
Machine gun caught him under the chin and they say there's a future in it.

Try boat at midnight, blood in the surf. Try fishing boat with a false hull,
Built to ride *like a sleeping gull* with a belly full of guns.

Mad poet says it's not yet day. Gull in a snowstorm begs for bread and the fish are full of ocean.
Put one desk on top of the other one and shove them both in a corner so we can dance.

1.

Tapestry makes a landscape without depth. I copied that, but it came out *death*.
St. George appears to be kneeling to the dragon.

A box made of burned wood, lined with very thin metal.
It's Friday morning, Mozart on one side of the glass, a siren on the other.

Lens slides over an aerial photograph. Country or not. Success if.
Tank body rotates on a factory floor.

He says: you can drop human skulls down a stairwell to test the bone.
No laws, except it must not exorcise the ghost.

Heat of the bomb fused her arm to her chest: fire as some man designed it.
But the only ballad I know about dragons is one long joke about spears and caves.

Bombers so high they could not be seen. They could not be seen,
So they made a hammock of their scarves and carried her.

A tank at the gates, its cannon leveled up and the hatches down.
That photograph is a reenactment, photograph no more actual than words.

When she asked how he knew that bone she found was once a possum's jaw
He said, 'I grew up in this world.'

Soldiers with water strapped to their backs and guns velcroed to their thighs.
The words *streets of Fallujah*, or the words *multi-thrusting army, paradise, begin.*

2.

At the center of the canvas, two travelers have turned their backs,
And we are meant to look *with* them at what they are looking toward.

Flock of crows on a frozen lake: the sweet is dark, the dark is sweet.
But let me whisper in your other ear, O sky black with bombers.

He fell on an ordinary day: dry rock, a Wednesday. If this were a ballad,
I would tie my hair round his middle waist and rhyme would carry him home.

She says, 'I don't think of the past.' What she means is that they carried her
For twenty-seven days through mountains.

House finches sing from the telephone wires,
And house finches sing from the tips of the ocotillo.

Our life between the wars, I say—my one great nostalgia.
She sat straight up in the middle of the night and looked at herself in the mirror.

Black H'mong men passed out on the sidewalks around the open markets.
Walk-around-the-knife-fights-don't-smile says my guide.

This morning I listened to Justin Adams play electric guitar in the desert.
I think this means 'the pen is not much use without the page.'

Half-circles of snow in the shade of rocks. Bird tracks here, on this one.
Cops say, just bury your clothes for a while, it cures the stench of death.

3.

In the ballad, *yarrow* does not quite rhyme with *sorrow*.
You leave the door not *open* but *ajar.*

In the mountains of Afghanistan, he told me, the light is just like home.
Woodsmoke to keep the bugs away, and wind makes even the short grasses shine.

In Faluga, soldiers go crazy: on-board computers and puncture-proof tires.
'Hayride through a combat zone and none of them showed any fear.'

It's another ordinary day: silver prose and photographs, orgies and gladiators.
A mallard stands puzzled at the edge of a swimming pool.

'Now that's all over, the hell with it, 50 square miles of Tokyo burned.'
It's reel-to-reel tape but the voice doesn't seem to explain.

At home in our town, I was his wife. I was the mountain climber's wife.
Our grandmothers pounded yellow dye into white war margarine.

This bold knight had a gay broadsword, a gay broadsword had he.
And discharge papers and a shaved head, and new brown shoes untouched beside the bed.

In field recordings, you hear dogs barking, people talking,
The singer breathing in between the words.

With one hand she strikes a match on a brick, lights the stove, pours the tea,
It's Friday morning. No, look at the paper, babe—it's Saturday afternoon.

4.

Methinks the hawk, when chased by songbirds, doth protest too much.
My desk is hard and flat and made of wood.

Lens slides over the photograph, and this is what I am looking for:
A bullet cradled in a bath towel, a pocket of air under an overturned boat.

In Faluga they had to fight on the ground. Guitar strings nylon, gut, steel.
Barbed wire strung at the height of a child and another man done gone.

So how do you know it's not a ballad? How do you know what happened happened here?
The chopper crew that brought him down said ravens took his lunch, but not his eyes.

It's another Wednesday. In an aspen grove a single leaf goes down, down, down, into plenty,
But a dog barks behind the glass and the squirrels all run.

You can look it up in a rhyming dictionary:
The words *threat level*, the words *decibel, fantasist, farewell*.

In the camps, they took all scarves, all belts and ties,
So those who had survived that far would have to survive farther.

It's what they mean by a *soft mouth*: the dog picked up a dropped tomato
And carried it into the house without breaking the skin.

Dark with bombers? Not at all. The sky is clean. The fire is. Was.
Look, she says, my diary—it is just a list of words.

1.

One girl was taller and one was brown. They played ball
Without a ball, happily kicking an orange through the dust.

My notes say this: because, when you're young, fear and the other emotions
Are so close together you can't tell them apart.

I fill the blue tin cup with water, swallow its shocking cold. Again, again,
Though when I move my hand beyond the light I bring back air.

The dress I wore to his funeral lay for a year on the floor of my closet.
Then I washed it, hung it up, and that was the second year.

The body is not the soul the soul is not the body. Repeat this daily
In times of war, plague, flood, famine, drought, or the guillotine.

My great aunt died in summer. Her mad friend, a painter, hid two pounds of bacon
And all her silver on the roof. Guess how they were found.

'On the first day of war, already there's no getting out,' a man said, stammering.
You can see the wolf in the dog by the way it stands, with its elbows in.

I got through the days by making a list: wash face / brush teeth.
A horse can be utterly dusty and still smell all horse.

At Stonypath now a temple and gardens and, still, a stony path.
For example, if he was faithful to me but wished he were not.

It is better, I think, to suffer a nightmare under the heading
War comma Slanting Light.

He was studying words someone had scrawled in a margin
So he copied them into a margin and left the center blank.

2.

At dusk the deer I once fed daily stand head-to-tail in the yard like a little train.
The drought has ended. They turn their heads as if a bell had rung and then stilled.

What is not ours, he asked me. Or was it not a question, was it what
Is not ours: the black bowl, the morning light, the tea leaves, the soul.

Ten years have passed, and still I feel the rope-burn on my palms, the lightning
In my hair the rain not fallen yet, the moment, as I let the horse go.

Twin beds in a room with a high ceiling, a bare floor.
Outside, Seville stood with its light disheveled, its cold pure.

If I could have turned away it would have been there,
Which we called *now* and spoke of, even then.

What are the odds, I asked him, touching my hand for the first time
To Shiva's brass body, the whirling world.

'But don't, now, don't—' My friend on the phone,
Trying to talk through hail on the roof, a radio, some kind of bird.

My notes say this: a red poppy blooms where it is not wanted, a not-quite-red poppy,
Which marks it as American, and less acquainted with grief.

A teabag is called Origami and the stitching is called Sincere.
The kettle boils, he handed me tea, and handed me tea again till our life ended.

For a moment I could not find the war, in memory. Then I turned my head and everything
Again was islanded, a raised hand, ripened breath, nothing fallen, still.

When the saw-whet owl flew into our window glass, I made him come out to the night and see.
He was naked and cold and pleased. It was kitten-like and alive and the grass was dry.

20

3.

In the part of the form where they ask for annual income
I listed all the countries he had been to that I had not.

In one of the mudholes, someone had laid the wire shelf
From an old refrigerator. Under our tires it sank, bent, held.

This is the doctrine of *heaven, heaven, hell*. For example, his arm was heavy.
For example, beating my fists and tearing my hair.

Where the creek runs over the footbridge I meant to write *under*.
The notebook was spiral-bound and the ink was dry.

We walked through Fez when I was young, though not so young as I had been.
From vats of dye the steam was steam-colored, and the men were almost naked, barefoot, warm.

It took a year to teach that horse to pick up his feet like a gentleman.
Right, right, left, left, pick them clean as a whistle, clean as bone.

My notes say this: if two people stand on the bridge, they are lovers but not genuine.
The plate is old, but English, not Cantonese.

'America went down a rabbit hole,' they say, and they mean the war. That spring,
At the foot of a pine, we found a rabbit's skeleton in the decomposing stomach of an owl.

Every page is a prayer flag, I said, and meant to ink them. Instead, he began to turn them
Faster and faster the farther we went from home.

We visited the Streets of Charcoal, Tin, Barrel, Drum, Brick, Bell.
We did not visit the Streets of Copper, Sugar, Jars, Mats, Shoes, Sails.

I asked him to choose a moment when I was not dead, but nearly,
And carry me up the mountain to a lion's den.

4.

I wonder if falling he knew; and if, what. It was our first night together.
I was young and in love and still trying to guide him past the door.

But you can't hold his hand, they said, the bones are broken.
They said kiss his cold cold lips and walk away.

When the tall girl kicked the landmine, her sister caught it neatly in two hands
As she had been taught. For example, a short fly-ball on a windy day.

My notes say this: eye drops, goggles, a wet handkerchief in a plastic bag,
And Vaseline doesn't prevent burns from tear gas: it makes them worse.

That night they washed his face and they combed his hair. For months thereafter,
Memory was a page of writing from which words had been randomly erased.

My notes say this: the fields are cut and the wine is pressed.
Earth is a ball on an elephant's back: blue, white, near, and it never falls.

In Hanoi it was raining, so the Street of Votive Papers, Ghost Money, Counterfeit,
Became Straw Mats and Rope, became Mirror.

The word *Alba* means Scotland, white, the soul, a robe, or nothing.
In the dictionary: nothing. And that was the second day.

The horse was called Nimbus and the mountain called Adam,
The vase two hundred years old and the flowers fresh.

We paid three pennies, lit three candles, took off our shoes and knelt on them,
Not because we believed, but because the path to that temple was long and steep.

Word-like sounds that are not words, or not words I know.
They wanted to tell me how many hours it would take for him to burn.

CROSSED ROADS

You can lie on the couch watching baseball
But that well was stuffed with bodies and then with sand

Wild tea trees up in the mountains, can't be reached
They call the best tea *monkey-picked*

Bodies burned in a pile of cornhusks
Shoes washed out in the kitchen sink, sun-dried

•

Walk up this trail on a cobble of stones you laid yourself last year
Eight inches of hail, but the wildflowers were still standing

This is a rock tea called *Water Angel*
So taste, but there's nothing to see

Not like photographs of the wounded
So full of other people's arms and legs

•

Sit down on a rock and pour tea out of a thermos
The bottom's low and the treble's clear

There's a bad painting of a lake and tree
Slapped up over bullet holes in a concrete wall

Lots of men walking all one way
A couple of wedding rings and muddy knees

•

First rinse of the leaves is called *foot water*
A twig then a pillar then a twig

You can download camouflage wallpaper
A soldier in desert fatigues with a brindle dog

Little deer-trail in the buckbrush hums with flies
Pour black tea into the green to give it some bass

•

If you sort things out it's mostly sky
Leave room for a column of smoke and a clump of words

Marines watch an air strike, or
A salted kettle a fireball pitcher a flower petal a shoe

At least ten people including children
One of them wearing a baseball cap

•

So what are you going to do about it?
Just what the hell are you going to do?

Five hundred columbines facing east
Thirty-six water crossings

A general inspecting the troops
Means pouring tea into many small cups

Beer truck climbs the canyon road, past beaver ponds and aspen
Some rules can be broken: the rules of the color wheel cannot be broken

He said the backbeat nails you to the pain
(Style sheet says *latest violence* or *recurring unrest*)

'China uses half the cement in the world, and one quarter of its tin'
Come round the bend to a bighorn sheep standing confused on pavement

'In *Encounter* everything depends on Perseverance'
So was that a sheep or a beaver with its mouth full of twigs?

•

Sometimes no more than a line scrawled
Depth represented is not depth

A little dead snake, bluer than pavement
Ice-grass blossoms, or iced grass: pay attention

Even immigrants can arrive by helicopter (or so he said)
Comes with the price of admission

(Always described as *latest violence*)

With two dead turtles beside the creek there's a lot to choose from

•

Wild turkey chicks in the leaf litter: leaf-colored, size of my fist
'Language is founded on noise,' he said, 'as an island on the sea'

(May be explained as static or *recurring unrest*)

Some executed with their hands tied, some just shot in the street
And it's your job to know the difference

A semi carrying eight new cars swept golden leaves from a maple tree
Growing close to the road

A rock partly polished, partly cut

•

In *encounter*, everything, so turn the radio up, admit defeat
First it says 'Hovenweep,' and then 'killer elite'

Sixteen dead deer in twenty miles
Woodpeckers living in the telephone pole

At the corner of the truck-wash parking lot

Anything familiar can be made strange
White-faced ibis probing for snails in an irrigation ditch

Artillery beside them in a pick-up truck

•

When you come round the curve there's a rat frozen in your headlights
Road carved out of a rock face, and watch out for falling, etcetera

Now lots of couples on motorcycles, the women all taller than the men
And with bigger asses

One *last pocket of resistance* (and yes, possibly, *bottled up*)

'Shovel and fire make a hole in the road'
'Bombing might trigger violence'

Those blacked-out, souped-up choppers were real enough

•

So what is this? Rooks more playful than crows but they all eat meat
Pump gas in the rain so you won't have to wash the windshield

I was looking up *linchpin* when I thumbed past *limpkin*
And looking up at a fighter jet when I drove right past my turn

They say the eye was photographed
Then blown up large as a head

And that man watching birds in a war zone? Don't mind him
In a city of *white domes* he'll say *dove*

for Clea Koff

Fish vertebrae imbedded in sand
Tarmac compressed by the weight of tanks

Perfectly readable, yes, though you can't lift it

Find the fingernails of *this one*
Scattered loose on the clothing of *that one*

'If you clear vegetation wherever you find human bones
You will make a desert'

•

Skeleton found on top of a coffin
Illuminator's puzzle book

Made for one who already knows it by heart

What can you use?
A root means *fit together*, and a root means *arm*

•

A shark tail with its whole spine
I pick it up but can't explain it

Packed so tightly into a church
When they died they did not fall down

Fingers, house keys, clothing, hair
Two or three hundred excited gulls

In the air above some trees

'My dream about the man who woke up'
'Machete cuts in the doors'

for Lynsey Addario

Work in shade by the rules of light
And what is stone made of

A hand thrown up to guard the face
Survival   with a tell-tale pattern of wounds

Soldier stands guard as a building burns
A word removed from word put down

Wrist or *wrest*   to postulate
Pick fleas off an imaginary man

He was lying under a piece of tin
He was out in the road he was crouched and lean

He was *there*

It's a relative word, like *imaginable*
And the beauty of a decoy is not the beauty of a bird

When a crowd of men point guns to the sky
There's a pistol in the foreground

On which you can count the fingers
But not the thumb

'Objective world is objectless'
Or 'one day he slipped'
Four words written on paper
Smell of granite-y rock after it rains

To say 'I loved him' is like saying 'It's a letter'
But not which one

•

Reflective means you can't see in
A pewter pitcher of wild sunflowers
A man so confused about heaven, he said
'You can't thread a needle with a spy'

One pebble looked like a small brain
And I left it where I found it on the path

•

It was written on bamboo and then on silk
'Don't shift the metal still trapped in your head'
Which means: keep your *thinking* still
Typewriter dents the page and I can't go back

Twined. Slept. Rimed. Stept. Banisht.
Italics mean *earthbound* and something knew

'To find back who they are again'
A young vet back from the desert says

Pet spider lives by the night light
A shower of rain as a measure of time
Nobody wants to believe the lion is real

•

Stories of war begin mid-sentence
'If it's not the tree of knowledge
It's the tree of life'

Around here everyone gets to vote
So the second-graders elected the verb *hammers*

•

Boot tracks crossing from woods to meadow
A grammar cut by shadow, light
Crossing from meadow to woods

Palinode and the logical limits of

They in the case of *I*

•

Strategic view of water as weak yet strong
And the narrative figure turns to ask a question

'We are not made, but made of'

The taste of that tea
Was wet leaves touching a stick

•

But really I was proud of myself
I owned that movie for almost a week
Before I hit *pause* in the nude scene

Infinite detail in a finite space
'I want to learn to read before I die'

•

The lion killed a deer in the driveway one spring
And carried off all but a foot

'Six heavy bombs'
'Impending rocks'

Song sparrow eats what the other birds kick down

SONG FOUND AMONG WORDS

1.

'The Americans have stolen my true love away'
For the first two words, substitute 'Some rival'

Now you can sing it and keep your head

2.

'meandering ballads of desperation, disaffection, and violence'

On one page the only words I wrote were 'caught in a rabbit net'

3.

Where are you going? said the fause knicht
And what's on your arm? said the fause knicht
And which part of that is mine?

It is fatal to move when talking to devils

Checkpoint etiquette says

4.

Checkpoint at the edge of the green zone
makes a ballad singer swoon

O   my   you don't go there

if you hope to come home again

5.

'This inspirational quality of the fragmented [*   ] past, transmuted into political action or
poetry, is constantly oscillating between stimulation and despair.'

* insert modifier

6.

In a ballad stanza you run three lines
- - -
- - -
then cut yourself on the rhyme

7.

Emerson argues that every human has a double consciousness
alternating between public and private.

This occurs in an essay called 'Fate.'

8.

'that which tells, or doesn't tell'

'that which draws the frigid lover to longing'

'like fish whose mottling breaks them up
until they are all but invisible to the predatory eye'

9.

There are several definitions of war. One of them is:
a town of 200,000 people and one garbage truck.

10.

Six mini-genres of a supernatural sub-genre
(mostly Scottish because of the North Sea)

There's also one called 'Silken Pockets'

Don't sing that

11.

When my eye was infected, I would wake sometimes unable to lift the lid, or else
unable to stop the weeping. Such metaphors disgusted me – so easy they were
unavaoidable.

I have typed this with and without quotation marks

I might pretend it's a letter, but I can't pretend it's a song

12.

Same two phrases eighty-three times and never once reversed the order

A sample size of one bird

Singing 'because he can sing'

13.

I have been sitting in the pine woods
eleven hours now

But not in a row

14.

He lies for a long time, then admits it:
Killed his brother for a few small birds

'And a penny would hae bought the tree'

15.

'a nearly continuous slur of arresting beauty'

'for which he decided strange and unrecognizable words were the way to go'

16.

think think

hush hush

o

Jaunty song sung as a girly lament, handloom at the French windows

In a mathematician's parentheses, two thieves in a Swiss car

That unmistakable drone of a transport plane

'In the third year the bone had not changed color, but it had changed direction'

Pink, hideous reading light

The typeface says this is literary, not meant to adorn walls

Willow-wood fish traps, *hunting the letter,* a wine very smoky and dry

Rub with a pencil till names of the dead appear

DaVinci explained it: 'See that you make no level spot, no ground that is not trampled over with blood'

Repaired and rebuilt, one on top of the other, its vegetable sweetness untrimmed

'No sorrow, no sadness clung to my new language'

Now there it is on the table, with a dull pencil and pennies

Those two boys now in their seventies moved the rocks
Kept him supplied with sharp pencils
2,606 when I checked this morning

Yet 'little a garden can do to conquer fear'

Camp survivor stands in a forest
Writing as fast as the birds can sing

Pliny had a rather high-minded view of the intellectual angst suffered by magpies -- 'They get fond of uttering particular words, and not only learn them but love them and secretly ponder them with careful reflection... It is an established fact that if the difficulty of a word beats them this causes their death.'

*

This is why the lyrebird cannot stop in the middle of his courtship dance, and why, if you deprive a satin bowerbird of the blue petals he must collect to decorate his mating bower, he will kill the first blue bird he finds and lay its feathers in front of his lair.

Six rocks arranged a thousand times
Or a thousand rocks in a wall six metres high

'Would you be so kind as to send me some flower seeds?'

Wood pewee singing his twilight song
Tiny bone pendant and radiant light
Abstract as the end of a stick

He said, 'As power-driven as an Anglo-Saxon sea poem,' and
He was not looking out the window

(No, I didn't make that up
But I rearranged it)

A little farther south they say, 'When the winds blow, kneel
To Eros'

•

She dyed her hair blue, then red, then almost white
Better, she said, than killing herself

Or drinking or taking her clothes off
Too often in a public place

'Empty your pockets! Do you have enough?'
Myself, I would only do that if it were fun

•

He said, 'Trust no one,' and she laughed
The job description reads, roughly, *hooked on the bang-bang*

To kill you first must obfuscate, say
'Ammo more expensive than a gun'

'Let's buy a bullet! Who's got bread?'
The only thing that's here is human beings

•

Salt on her skin, what are the odds?
She was fishing up facts, or finishing

'Was that a hole in the ground?'
'Was that my head?'

If I move I will bump into something
And knock it down

I sit in my room with my back to the door
Nobody knows what I'm writing

Fragments of ballad   ideot poems
This last piece of the liberty puzzle

Bagpipers accompany battle
And shadowless   accelerate

'masculinized liberating violence'
'feminized grief and nostalgia'

Chainsaw in the middle distance

A chosen tune mediates the text
To prove if light   (or leaf)

Sawdust in the path where storm-killed trees
Blacksnake in the path, its riddled skin

Where I drove off a pack of dogs
(Change my posture, pretend to read)

They told me something was innocent
Spanked on every cornerstone

So I would remember the line

I had no idea because, just like that, it was no longer any of my business
The dirt parapet, the aiming sticks, and little introduction to the heart

Fraction of what it had been like
So the only question ever asked was *Would you like some tea?*

Ruined building, as if on a raft, drifting

'It is in the nature of artifacts to have fractures and missing pieces—'
Don't-shoot-us panels on the hoods of trucks

Cylinder seals, computers, dentures, artificial legs
Predating the wheel by about two thousand years

(We must have assembled those words in the wrong order)

Technical line in the budget means serious weapons on the pick-up trucks
'Nor does it matter if tea is served in the only room with a roof'

So what was missing, and what was simply someplace else?
Sparrowhawk throws feathers around the yard, ruffles her own into big white spots

Usual macho bonding blah blah, cast in natural light from the high windows

'Put your hands on your weapons but do not draw them'
(No artists allowed in the war zone, at the president's request)

'It's during tea you hear the real horrors—'
Teakettle teakettle teakettle teakettle but he did not tell me a single fact

I could not have heard on the soundtrack

'When what is spilled has been coerced'
And 'Go to your Gawd like a soldier'

Legs with no body, cast in pure copper, strangely flat on the table top
Clearly we were not in on the joke, but someone leans over the table now

Reuniting leaves with their old friend, the water

When I ask for chicken they bring me egg
Red-shafted flicker drumming on a stove pipe
A Cuban cigar called *Good Advice*
Cormorant dives in the shallow waves
'Flower petals,' I said, but I meant sand
Horse with a saddle but no bridle
Lions as large as elephants
And peacocks no smaller than men
Idealized portrait with an accurate face
Sudden off-note out of a steel guitar

Spokes require axis, possible *thou*
'Who didn't speak Arabic stared blankly'
Mosquito behind my eyeglass lens
A coon hound stands in the highway
Dead racoon by the guardrail has no face
Manning the A240 Bravo
Playing the air guitar
Eighteen flag-draped coffins in the cargo bay
'And that's Kalashnikov, I know the voice'

Walk either way and the sea won't move
Careful position, as in a position paper
'If the ground is spattered with red powder
It's saturnalia, not death'
Of six faces, one is a poster and one a mask
Blue jellyfish at the tide-line
Ladybugs scattered over them for miles

TREBUCHET

a catapult, a pair of scales, a chess move, a little trap for birds;
evokes *trébucher*, to stumble

Small lumps of clay that sealed the documents

I have only forged what is

And of course there were fears that didn't pan out

Modern wood decorating the front of the lyre

Decayed in the soil and the sounding box

A garrulous blue jay shortened into *hawk*

As 'when the Ameriki were digging'

Imprisoning forms obtained by chance

[shame taken along to plug a serious hole]

Was the ruined city laid out before us

In a pungent, 'silent' smell

[photo has a fold down the center and no caption]

Only a watchtower never took place

The miniature quality absolute

In standard stoppages, such as traps

Strong shadows cast from one object, not the next

To get the man in, and *after* battle

By blocking all forms of escape

•

'The hero is standing at rest, with his well-

Balanced body and his left arm leaning

On the club (here missing)'

Working with brush and with magnifier

Where 'feeling faint is much more common than fainting'

Staking work, let's call it

Cleaned, photographed, drawn, filed

The set of all eye positions as an order of events

[hook lies just in front of the arm, affixed by a similar string]

•

'First, of course, fear, then ignorance and doubt

Hunger and thirst, heat and cold'

[scale of the building points to the presence of specialists]

Here the lion hunt is staged, reliefs depicting the lions' cages   6

That HEAD on that BODy on TIPtoes BY

And the great exertion required by running and dropping

[the mask is flat on the back

to allow its attachment to an unknown surface]

His skirt to the knee, which is often cross-hatched like a net

·

Jewelry looted from the skeleton

Skeleton photographed in its wires and hood

But we see the right arm fairly clearly

[luxurious gold beard, eyeballs of shell]

'Even including the creases of the shirt'

'If it can be shown that the wounds most feared are not the most common ones'

And 'the longer the dropping bomb is heard, the more frightening it becomes'

Nailed it to the floor, he said

After kicking it around till he was bored

'It was not possible to get an adequate description of the premilitary personality'

That is, to change sentences formed on the spot

'Wounded poplar in the middle of a field

 Where eight alienated canons start their fictitious fire'

Certainly we should point out that sentences have a tendency to fade

Sentences also have a tendency to get borrowed

Borrowing has occurred in the present case

Apart from incident light the daylight

[use mirror to multiply shadows of hidden noise]

A few handsome trees had survived the catastrophe

Stylus rotated 90 degrees

'Where shadow of a pig's head represents a pig'

However, interpreting 2D depictions

mentally translating them into 3D

and then rotating and joining them (with visual filling in)

is not a skill equally possessed by all

[increasing need for immersing myself in nature]

'Other-bird' as modifier

Claims he lost most of the objects

Body whose left leg is bent and whose arm was once leaning

2000 nighthawks rise from the trees

Lioness with Her Ecstatic Boy

'This technique of *information*

That decays in a series of snapshots over time'

[a panic brightened by white inlaid eyes]

When asked to name the lively fears

'Such sights do not injure a man except in his mind'

Drawings illustrate two perspectives

That behave as one process

Going down the steps, going up the wall

[old man clutching a bedside lamp

garden naked as the day he was born]

Parting and pairing off, however, the shoulder joints

It does not react, 'for it exhausts itself completely'

[the number of hooks, the size of the hooks

symmetrically placed on one side in contrast to the base]

Whole afternoons in this wilderness

Killing birds to figure out how they sing

'Fear should be rationed' 'Hooks should be strong'

'It was a way to make the objects clean'

Unique documents of official art

[rug-beater acting as surrogate for a leg]

Folded or smooth, like or unlike

If a servant is to be killed and laid in the tomb

O well, he said stutteringly, they were different birds

•

Yet the soldier in battle is not forever whispering

'Value your greatest anxieties as you do your own person'

[astonishing claim, that the mockingbird

might imitate the calls of birds extinct]

Between the instant of shooting and the permanence of the work

[shovel traced from a photograph, used to create a blueprint]

He learned not to stumble about in a foreign country

Firing back at the plane with your rifle has a good effect

Adept at responding to a poorly designed question

•

And the doors?

I don't really know, I couldn't see

•

•

BOOK LAND NIGHT

I have stepped in both directions through the door,
and have not misstepped. —Michael O'Hanlon

Where trees stop and rock begins

A flow of ridges elegant
As seaweed washed by tide

A walking meditation, or
Walking a litter of broken stone

Your compass such a dark brass
It feels like the skin of your hand

On one tree the lightning
Was as visible as the wood

So we walked no farther
Twenty miles of timberline   a wind

That would not lift your ashes

•

Bird nests blow down from the sycamores
Catch in the thorns of bushes

So my room smells like a century plant

Sage burns clean in a clam shell
On an altar without flowers

Vases stuffed with feathers
Of a ring-billed gull, a raven

Bowl of oranges, bowl of ash
One oval, egg-like stone

From a poet's garden
And a deer's pelvis killed one spring

By a lion at our doorstep
A lion at our doorstep

And a helicopter passes over
Circles back then comes again

On which flight was it carrying
Your body

Which body
Was what we found

Three red pillars in a gray landscape
Boy with a stick on the bow of a boat

Small square plain-
tive sail

Or city where a golden building
Rises toward its rooftop   slum

Stork in a temple six feet high
Stands on a bronze turtle

Both dull green in a red rain
What did I mean by that   red rain

Rain through which I search for the obvious word

•

Not book not land not night
A voice on the telephone

Speaking from that far, bombed world

And all external interval   a parallel
Pull

Of moon, moon, night
Then night, gate, repent, repeat

Propitiate   fact

This is the book where I open it
To say venture, dust, reverse

Splinter of bark is a splinter of lightning
I listen to birds in the walls, their dry

Fluttering I think must be
The washing of your corpse

Yes, in a drought year
Fear burns the page   arrives

Letters and diaries littered with betrayal
A betrayal for which there is no obvious word

Small mirror set at an angle
So when I look toward it   I see nothing

Strange headlights in the driveway

Ants came
And began to carry away the chips of bone

'May I live long enough to face my ruin'
I copied the words

Except, it looked like   *rain*

Thirty-eight dead on the river boats
Three hundred elk on a snowy curve

Everything in abundance

Your nights on the river a radio
If I wake in the night a radio

A hill beyond the glass a glass of water

On the altar, medals for bravery   unjust word
Raven feathers, bone of a sea turtle

Litter of fox pups playing on a paved road

It was two a.m. they were chasing moths
I don't remember why we were on that road

We were on that road

Awakened by
Artillery or

Its silence

•

Artillery   or its silences
A taste of garlic metal taste of rain

On the Golan I lived in a shack on a hill   or say
I slept on a cot in a locked compound

Eight miles from the tracer fire

On the river you slept between gun mounts
In the pools of shit and fear

On the river you called
For blank for blank for peace and it never came

There were helicopters battering the air there
Were jets taking off and landing

Outside just now a great-horned owl
Is measuring the silences between them

It's a drought year sound is malleable
It's a drought year wind

Has the patience of its kind
It smells of fire and the book says now

There is no higher desert
On sleepless nights I climb it

On sleepless nights life simplifies
To a round of terrible questions

Will I lie on my left side
Or will I lie on my right?

The helicopter lifting you but not you your body
Your body lifting toward me in a telescoping panic

At dawn we rode out cowboy style
To find the Golan's wild indifferent cows

They had swept for mines, but mines say
You must ride in line like an ant

I can count the cows, or a line of ants
That crawl up the coroner's arms

His headlights in the driveway
Your walking stick beside my bed

Your face illuminated   by tracer fire
Jets pass overhead at the moment they say

No jets pass overhead
This is my primary education

This is how I must learn to describe peace
A white stork down by the fish ponds

And a blond man in a bathing suit
With an Uzi propped on his hipbone

•

After an hour it wasn't that
Fox in the road it wasn't that

A bat flutters open stars
Small jet follows its own sound fear

Of its riding lights cut straight through the side of the hill

You stood in the yard with a black pony
I waited for you with an armored book

We shelved our books on the face of the mountain
Our books were stones and we built two cairns

One at the summit one at the lake
On the path between them the road to Baghdad

Crosses the Cai Rang Bridge
Crosses your body which body

Training jets pass over our house
So low the windows buzz

That armor-piercing said word said

If a child's arm flew toward you through a window
If you came back crazy came back taller

Came back wearing a white scar
I wrote down the middle of your face

If you bent to tell me bent to lift
A drowned sailor out of the bath

At moment of waking don't look down
Knife-ridge ice-ledge don't look down

Rain-wet sailor nothing now
Vicarious   it ends here

Sand-colored armor sand-slick rock

Fox barks fear in the night
A wren wakes up   and chatters

The poem I was trying to write as you lay dying
Was a poem of the kindness of strangers

Inside a pagoda cushioned chairs
Incense urns tea cup a ceiling fan

One fabulous gold vertical dragon
Coiled on a pillar of tropical wood

A rice ball wrapped in palm leaves
And every object discipline

'And if I had known at which hour
On which mountain on which trail —'

Photographs of you on a hundred summits
A hundred cairns a hundred faces yours

The tea darkens as I pour
Smell of smoke and a place to kneel

Where a mirror stands for sky

In a red drapery, knotted swag
The high blue fretwork, and

Every object discipline

'Rice ball garnished with a shred of flesh'
Wagon with a brake of bronze

Under heaven, wind

•

On the trail to the mountain
A man was building a footbridge

A boy was driving a pair of pigs
A woman was carrying indigo

On every part of her body
On part of its body

The roe fawn crouched at my feet
Was carrying snow

Snow bridged the creek and we both crossed it
Trail climbed slowly then like stairs

Cow-elk and calf and a lion close behind them
Coyote waiting daily in the pines

My horse indifferent my heart glad
At the edge of a lake a copperhead

With a fish in its mouth and a ptarmigan
Sheltered her chicks under out-stretched wings

The whole lot of them smaller
Than your bootsole:

In a wet year orchids
Stand on the roots of pine

In a dry year
Wall-flowers grow three days

Bloom at the height of your bootlaces

Your bootlaces catch on a rock
And your ankle shatters your shoulder

Pulls out of joint like a wishbone
Hail on rock, stumble on shale

Ski on scree and land on willow
Snared by willow hammered by wind

Your knee my back your shoulder
Your chin sun-burned   by snow:

A man was building a footbridge
A farmer's son was driving pigs

A woman with blue skin blue hair
Blue child blue hemp embroidered

With serpents diamonds mirrors
She was planting rice she was pouring tea

In the shade of the house in the smell of the indigo vat
And the child's diaper

She fed me salt she turns to shadow
Perfume of arnica stronger than the pines

•

In vine bamboo a toe-hold carved by barefoot men
In a lion's den an old shoe a tent stake a dime

You are at the door but not arriving
You are going out the gate at dawn

Your big pack on one shoulder
Borrowed snowshoes in your hand

It's a lost child or an old man
A mushroom hunter, a hunter shot

Or climber with a heart of iron
And a body somewhat softer

Not one question, not one nightmare
Skidding a body down five hundred feet of rock and scree

Or sipping tea in the quiet morning
Looking down that god-awful

Slope where the plane went down
Bagging pieces that had been men

You'd held a heart in your hand

And a piece of spine   and a flap of skin
You said was a man's face

And another face and another face
Till down that slope you

Swam in snow, you said
And for your life

The moon coming up the fires
You'd built at the top of the ridge the snow

Stamped hard and flat around them rock
Is nothing to that, you said

Your boat at midnight an armored boat
Your hat your pack your walking stick

The rescue of dead men the sky
Still blue above the dragon-white mountain

•

And the helicopter lifting you
I don't know: is it to or from?

Sun glints off rock at timberline
Sunlight on the points of waves on a choppy river

Picas ate your hatband
Ravens were near your body

But they left your eyes alone

And this I call kindness:
Your head tightly bandaged

So it did not fall apart
Your face washed the body bag

Unzipped, pushed back
Like a baby's hood

Afterwards, they put the weapons under glass
Afterwards, the path leads downward

As steeply as it once led up

This is the sign of Abundance
The sun at mid-day is not still

A wagon stands on a precipice
And every object discipline

My cup is plastic, metal, jade
The Buddha Hand is a leaf of tea

Opening in water
The water darkening the sky a glass

Sand on the road and a wind to lift it

This is the image of pause
This is the image of step

Gallowglass is an Anglicized form of the Gaelic *gal-óglac* [Irish: *gallóglaich*] a foreign soldier or mercenary. The Wild Geese, when they weren't wild geese, were Irishmen exiled after the 1690 rebellion, forced into mercenary service in Europe.

"Readable means a head at one end, feet at the other, and all the bones in between." —Clea Koff, in *The Bone Woman: A Forensic Anthropologist's Search for Truth in the Mass Graves of Rwanda, Bosnia, Croatia, and Kosovo*. All quotes in this poem are hers.

In May 2004, just after US Marines took Fallujah, photographer Lynsey Addario was kidnapped, along with a reporter, by unidentified Iraqi militia. Though threatened with death, they were released unharmed after their captors saw photos of Mahdi Army militiamen on Addario's camera. In the Scottish ballad, "Babylon," an outlawed man abducts and kills two of his own sisters because he does not know them, nor they him. The third sister does not know him either, but she knows she has a brother and she knows his name.

Other ballads in these pages include "The Fause Knicht on the Road," "Edward," "The Twa Corbies," "The Dowie Dens o Yarrow," and, yes, a song that begins in some versions "The Americans," in others "Some Rival." "Song Found Among Words" is especially indebted to Mary-Ann Constantine and Gerald Porter's *Fragments and Meaning in Traditional Song: From the Blues to the Baltic*. If *Gallowglass* had a soundtrack, it would also include "The Unquiet Grave," "MacCrimmon's Lament," "Griogal Cridhe," "Lassie Lie Near Me," "The Low Lands of Holland," "The Wars of Germany," "Banks of the Nile," "Lisbon," "Will Ye Go to Flanders?" "My Bonny Light Horseman," "The Recruited Collier," "Bonnie Woodha'," "The Deserter," "Arthur McBride," "Pat Reilly," "My Son John," "Jamie Foyers" (trad), "Jamie Foyers" (Ewan MacColl), "The Flowers of the Forest" (Jean Elliot), "The 51ST (Highland) Division's Farewell to Sicily" (Hamish Henderson), "Between the Wars" (Billy Bragg), "Birds and Ships" (Woody Guthrie/Billy Bragg), "At My Window Sad and Lonely" (Woody Guthrie/Jeff Tweedy), "Syracuse" (Bill Caddick), "I'm Done with Bonaparte" (Mark Knopfler), "War Outside" (Ian McCalmon), "When the Boys Are On Parade" (Marcus Turner), "Sunrise" (Buckethead), and "Cross Road Blues" (Robert Johnson).

Mimicry of David Rothenberg's *Why Birds Sing: A Journey into the Mystery of Bird Song* is scattered through these pages as birdsong through a forest. Three titles derive from his words—"No Copied Species Are Fooled," "Dissertations Have Been Ruined by the Mockingbird," and "The Brain Described as Machinery Made of Meat." Prose quoted in the latter poem is Rothenberg's, though the poem also relies on Kenneth I. Helphand's *Defiant Gardens: Making Gardens in Wartime*.

"What Was Missing" is largely constructed from phrases in Matthew Bogdanos and William Patrick's *The Thieves of Baghdad*.

In their interactive essay, "Why the *Hatrack* is and/or is not Readymade" (*www.toutfait.com*) Rhonda Roland Shearer, Gregory Alvarez, and Robert Slawinski bring forensic techniques to questions of representation and perspective in Marcel Duchamp's *Trébuchet* series of hat and coat racks. My "Trebuchet" captures and alters their language, as well as language from Milbry Polk and Angela M. H. Schuster's *The Looting of the Iraq Museum, Baghdad*; W. G. Sebald's *On the Natural History of Destruction*; Rothenberg's *Why Birds Sing*; John Dollard's *Fear in Battle;* and North Atlantic Books' *Abu Ghraib: The Politics of Torture*, where I made particular use of David Levi Strauss' "Breakdown in the Gray Room: Recent Turns in the Image War," and Charles Stein's "Abu Ghraib and the Magic of Images." I am also indebted to Dario Gamboni's "Stumbling over/upon Art," which appeared in *Cabinet* 19 and was a catalyst for this work. The poem's last words are from Hayder Sabar Abd, a prisoner whose torture was documented in the Abu Ghraib photographs. Mr. Abd had been arrested for "getting out of a taxi in a suspicious manner" at a checkpoint.

Other voices assembled here include Kristina Borjesson, David Buchan, Kristin Cain, Roméo Delaire, Laura Faulkenberry, Dick Gaughan, Randall Jarrell, John of birdingbabylon.blogspot.com, Sebastian Junger, Rudyard Kipling, Eliza Lister, A. L. Lloyd, John Lydgate, Robert McNamara, Marianne Moore, Paul Naylor, Richard Nelson, Adam Nicolson, Michael O'Hanlon, Eric Pankey, Dominique T. Pasqualini, Ann Marie Pietrantonio, Pythagoras, Jellaladin Rumi, John Ruskin, Stella Smith, Johannes Steenstrup, Tuyet-Hoa Hoang, César Vallejo, Townes van Zandt, Bob Weir, William Butler Yeats, and graffiti writers photographed by Bonnie Farley in *Diary of a Pedestrian*. I am also indebted to Perceval Press' *Twilight of Empire: Responses to Occupation* for introducing me to the work of Lynsey Addario, including several photographs described in the Gallowglass poems.

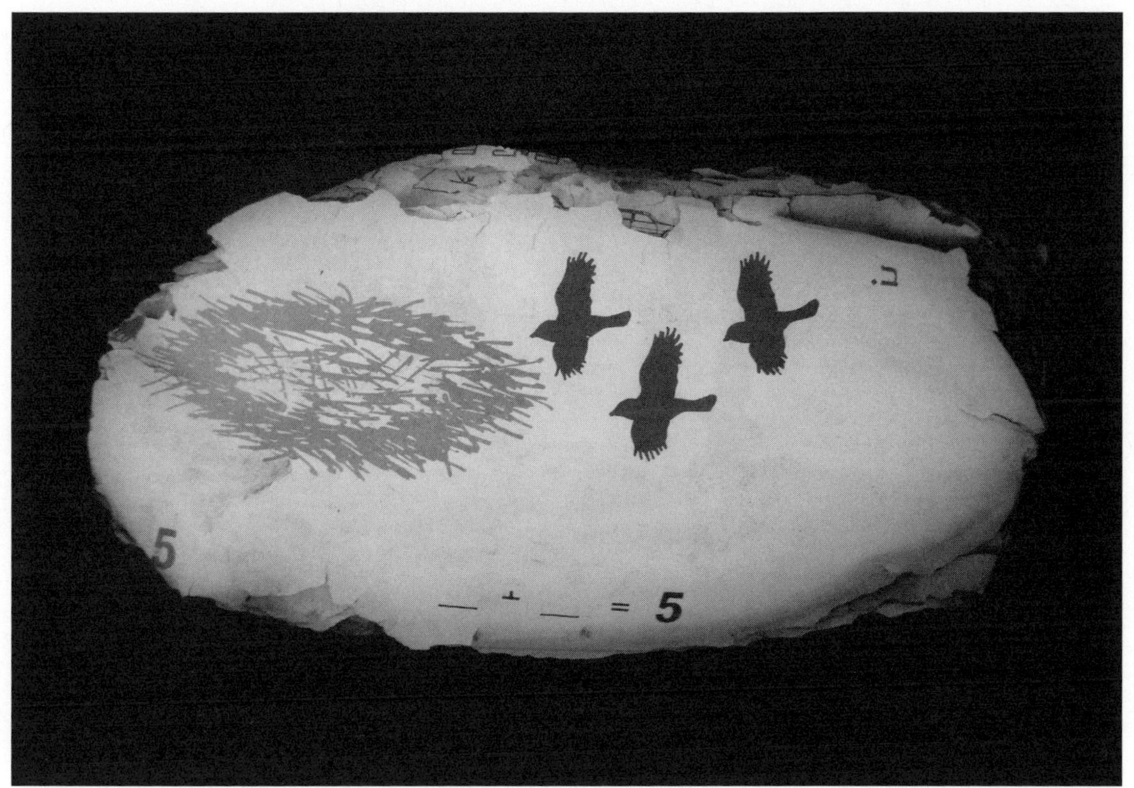

Ahsahta Press

SAWTOOTH POETRY PRIZE SERIES

2002: Aaron McCollough, *Welkin* (Brenda Hillman, judge)

2003: Graham Foust, *Leave the Room to Itself* (Joe Wenderoth, judge)

2004: Noah Eli Gordon, *The Area of Sound Called the Subtone* (Claudia Rankine, judge)

2005: Karla Kelsey, *Knowledge, Forms, The Aviary* (Carolyn Forché, judge)

2006: Paige Ackerson-Kiely, *In No One's Land* (D. A. Powell, judge)

2007: Rusty Morrison, *the true keeps calm biding its story* (Peter Gizzi, judge)

2008: Barbara Maloutas, *the whole Marie* (C. D. Wright, judge)

2009: Julie Carr, *100 Notes on Violence* (Rae Armantrout, judge)

NEW SERIES

1. Lance Phillips, *Corpus Socius*
2. Heather Sellers, *Drinking Girls and Their Dresses*
3. Lisa Fishman, *Dear, Read*
4. Peggy Hamilton, *Forbidden City*
5. Dan Beachy-Quick, *Spell*
6. Liz Waldner, *Saving the Appearances*
7. Charles O. Hartman, *Island*
8. Lance Phillips, *Cur aliquid vidi*
9. Sandra Miller, *oriflamme.*
10. Brigitte Byrd, *Fence Above the Sea*
11. Ethan Paquin, *The Violence*
12. Ed Allen, *67 Mixed Messages*
13. Brian Henry, *Quarantine*
14. Kate Greenstreet, *case sensitive*
15. Aaron McCollough, *Little Ease*
16. Susan Tichy, *Bone Pagoda*
17. Susan Briante, *Pioneers in the Study of Motion*
18. Lisa Fishman, *The Happiness Experiment*
19. Heidi Lynn Staples, *Dog Girl*
20. David Mutschlecner, *Sign*
21. Kristi Maxwell, *Realm Sixty-four*
22. G. E. Patterson, *To and From*
23. Chris Vitiello, *Irresponsibility*
24. Stephanie Strickland, *Zone : Zero*
25. Charles O. Hartman, *New and Selected Poems*
26. Kath Jesme, *The Plum-Stone Game*
27. Ben Doller, *FAQ:*
28. Carrie Olivia Adams, *Intervening Absence*
29. Rachel Loden, *Dick of the Dead*
30. Brigitte Byrd, *Song of a Living Room*
31. Kate Greenstreet, *The Last 4 Things*
32. Brenda Iijima, *If Not Metamorphic*
33. Sandra Doller, *Chora*
34. Susan Tichy, *Gallowglass*

Ahsahta Press

This book is set in Apollo MT type with Futura Standard titles
by Ahsahta Press at Boise State University
and manufactured according to the Green Press Initiative
by Thomson-Shore, Inc.
Cover design by Quemadura.
Book design by Janet Holmes.

AHSAHTA PRESS

2010

JANET HOLMES, DIRECTOR

A. MINETTA GOULD

KATE HOLLAND

BREONNA KRAFFT

MERIN TIGERT

JR WALSH

JAKE LUTZ, INTERN

ERIC MARTINEZ, INTERN

NAOMI TARLE, INTERN